The Power of Focus

Dr. Norman Thomas Jr.

Unless otherwise noted, all scripture is from the New King James Version of the Bible.

Scriptures marked KJV are taken from the King James Version (KJV): King James Version, public domain.

Scripture taken from The Message. Copyright © 1993, 1994, 1995, 1996, 2000, 2001, 2002. Used by permission of NavPress Publishing Group.

Scripture quotations marked New Living Translation are from the New Living Translation © 1996, 2004, 2007, 2013 by Tyndale House Foundation. Used by permission of Tyndale House Publishers Inc., Carol Stream, IL 60188. All rights reserved.

Scripture quotations marked New International Version®, NIV® Copyright ©1973, 1978, 1984, 2011 by Biblica, Inc.® Used by permission. All rights reserved worldwide.

The Power of Focus
By Dr. Norman Thomas Jr.

©2019 by Dr. Norman Thomas Jr.

ISBN: 978-1-7327062-1-7

Published by Norman Thomas Ministries | 3000 East Gauthier Road, Lake Charles, LA | www.NormanThomas.org

Editorial by Jordan Media Services | P.O. Box 761593
Fort Worth, Texas USA | www.jordanmediaservices.com

Design/Layout by Ken Fraser | www.impactbookdesigns.com

Printed in the United States of America. All rights reserved under International Copyright Law. No part of this book may be reproduced or transmitted in any form or by any means, electronic or mechanical, including photocopying, recording, or by any information storage and retrieval system, without the written permission of the publisher.

The Power of Focus

Leadership requires a high degree of focus. When focus is in operation, it provides clarity and precision, expedites the arrival of your desired outcome, and eliminates the pressure of temptation of anything that would prevent you from reaching your goal.

Because focus is so highly effective toward good leadership, the enemy's No. 1 objective is to rob you of it. There are many tools in the enemy's arsenal, but they all require your permission before they can successfully operate in your life. Among them is the force of distraction—the No. 1 opposing force of focus.

When focus is fully matured in one's life, provision will flow, clarity will emerge, and the exercise of mastery over the enemy will excel. All these qualities represent a major threat to the forces of life that oppose your success.

Distraction is the first level of attack against you. The enemy knows if he can distract you from anything related to your life assignment, you will never reach your destiny. This is his end goal!

As a leader, it's important to recognize when this is happening to you, and that you seek God for His wisdom—both in discerning those areas in which you are most likely to be distracted, and to reveal to you how to avoid or handle those distractions. Don't try to figure it out yourself. Instead, ask God for help. James 1:5 says, "If any of you lacks wisdom, let him ask of God, who gives to all liberally and without reproach, and it will be given to him."

Clarity and Precision

How important is it for you to have clarity and precision?

Clarity suggests you have a full and complete understanding of what it is you're doing, and where you desire to go. You have a plan, a strategy for getting from Point A to Point B, so that eventually you will have accomplished your goal.

Precision simply implies you operate with a degree of assurance and exactness in the instruction you follow to arrive at your goal. If your assignment lacks either of the two, then you won't reach the end goal. You'll miss the mark and you'll lack a sense of fulfillment.

We can see now why many leaders do not succeed. They may know their purpose, and they may even know how to accomplish their goals. However, what oftentimes is missing is a strategy for addressing the distractions that keep them from reaching their sense of focus.

When I was in high school, for example, I had a math teacher who loved to go fishing. As was his habit, he would often begin each class by telling one of his many fishing stories. It didn't take me or my classmates long to realize that, though he was a teacher by profession, this man loved fishing a lot more than he enjoyed teaching math.

How did that work against him?

One day, a student asked a question about fishing, and for about 30 minutes this man went on and on ranting about his fishing exploits—leaving only about 15 minutes to do what he was there to do, and that was to teach math.

Though he had clarity in what his assignment was, including knowledge of how to reach his end goal, the teacher obviously lacked the ability to carry out that assignment with precision. He became too easily enticed by the distraction of something other than his assignment, allowing it to dominate or control his focus. When we, as students, realized how easy this was to accomplish, we each took turns ensuring that he was lured away from his assignment each day.

Sadly, this is exactly how the enemy accesses your inability to stay on task. He will use cunning tricks to ensure that you are tempted, and subsequently enticed to look away from the thing you were created to be and do.

As a result, the teacher was not as effective

a leader as he could have been in teaching us the concepts of math.

When you don't project clarity and precision in leadership, it's inevitable that there will be a disruption of your ability to live and lead effectively. Focus ensures that you project the demeanor that is necessary to ensure the confidence of those who follow you.

People inherently desire good leadership, but where there appears to be a gap someone usually not qualified will inevitably rise to absorb what is perceived to be missing. This usually results in chaos or confusion. If you don't take charge of your destiny, counterfeit leadership is sure to rise in your life. You will end up subjected to people, places, and things that were never intended for your life. I like what the Bible says in Job 22:28, *New International Version:* "What you decide on will be done, and light will shine on your ways."

People will follow where and when there is clarity and precision in leadership. If you look behind you and no one is in sight, that's a clear indication that you may be missing these two important ingredients to focus.

The Benefits of Focus

Focus expedites the arrival to your desired outcome. You reach your end goal quicker because you don't allow distractions to get you off course. Focus eliminates anything that has the potential of interfering with your assignment or purpose—any temptation to yield, to stall, to procrastinate.

First Timothy 4:14-15, *King James Version,* says, "Neglect not the gift that is in thee, which was given thee by prophecy, with the laying on of the hands of the presbytery. Meditate upon these things; give thyself wholly to them; that thy profiting may appear to all."

The word *meditate* means, "to rehearse a thought" or "to contemplate on a particular matter." This translates to an ongoing focus and concentration that yields the benefit of progression and profitability. In other words, focus allows for the giving of one's self completely, with undivided and unbroken attention, to the task at hand. This is not something that happens accidentally or arbitrarily. Focus is highly intentional. It happens by design. You give yourself completely to it so that you may progress.

The quality of your focus is evident in the tangible manifestations it yields. It is safe to say that what you see around you is in direct proportion to those thoughts which are the subject of your focus. When your focus becomes Kingdom and purpose-related, there will be a reflection of such focus represented around you in physical form. Unfortunately, the opposite is also true. When there is no Kingdom or purpose-related focus, it will yield the fruit of natural, average, and ordinary living.

Read verse 15 from 1 Timothy, Chapter 4 again, only this time look at it in the *New International Version*. It says, "Be diligent in these matters; give yourself wholly to them, so that everyone may see your progress." What *matters* is this verse referring to? It's talking about the matters that concern one's assignment—those things you need to focus on.

Notice in this translation the word *meditate* is replaced with the word *diligent*. It says to be "*diligent* in these matters." Success is the outcome of diligent focus on the task at hand. One word often used to define diligence is *consistency*. Consistency implies unconditional committal without regard for adverse conditions or circumstances.

Ever wonder why some businesses prosper, and their assets are in the millions or billions of dollars, while others seem to flounder? The reason is simple: It's because one sets its sights on the outcome, diligently pursuing the end goal, while the other becomes distracted by forces assigned to abort or sabotage their success. In some cases, the assignment is not taken seriously. They become fixated with other opportunities that may not be designed for them, and lose focus of what they are really called to do.

When focus is in operation, you experience yet another benefit—ease.

Ease is developed over time as focus is practiced. When you're gifted to perform in a certain area, it fosters focus in that particular area of performance. This "ease" is an empowerment that propels you to fight the fight of faith and overcome EVERYTHING that stands in your way.

Whenever you fail to allow the power of focus to generate these benefits in your life, you become negligent in your assignment. Remember, biblical meditation provides you access to completion created by the giving of your complete and undivided attention to the task at hand. When you are meditating your assignment, you're envisioning and imagining the way it should be.

Singleness of Mind and Heart

Matthew 6:22-24 says, "The light of the body is the eye: if therefore thine eye be single, thy whole body shall be full of light. But if thine eye be evil, thy whole body shall be full of darkness. If therefore the light that is in thee be darkness, how great is that darkness! No man can serve two masters: for either he will hate the one, and love the other; or else he will hold to the one, and despise the other. Ye cannot serve God and mammon" (*King James Version*).

This Biblical truth is full of insight and revelation that opens certain laws of engagement when it comes to focus. If we had to summarize this excerpt from Jesus' teaching, we could call it "Singleness of Mind and Heart". The 'eye' given reference to here is not the physical socket in your head but rather the 'eye of the mind (spiritual eyes)' or the imagination of the heart. This is the conduit by which light (revelation) flows, darkness (ignorance) is minimized and focus is maximized. Your mind (the eye of your spirit) and your heart (your purposes, motivations, and intents) can only serve one master. You were never intended to operate with loyalty of heart and mind in two separate directions at the same time. This is what the Bible refers to as "double-mindedness," which yields one result; you will love one and despise the other. Unfortunately, when the mind and heart do not have a single focus, one will end up loving the wrong 'master'.

Double-mindedness creates chaos and confusion.

James 1:8, *King James Version,* says, "A double minded man *is* unstable in all his ways." In the *New Living Translation,* that verse says: "Their loyalty is divided between God and the world, and they are unstable in everything they do." In other words, the double-minded person is characteristic of indecisiveness and instability in every area of life.

Matthew 6:24, *New International Version,* says, "No one can serve two masters. Either you will hate the one and love the other, or you will be devoted to the one and despise the other. You cannot serve both God and money."

Just as no one can look in two directions at the same time, neither can you serve two masters at the same time. You cannot be married to the world and God. You cannot move forward and stay behind at the same time. One will succumb to the other.

Singleness of mind and heart provides understanding and insight into a thing. Double-mindedness creates confusion and delay of understanding. Without focus, you will lack the power of stability in thought and deed regarding any assignment. But when you allow focus to mature in your heart and mind, you avoid the dangers of double-mindedness.

Double-mindedness takes a toll on your mind to the degree that you never do anything for any significant amount of time before you jump to something else. From day to day, you are constantly moved by the wind of circumstances with no anchor to hold you in place. You lack the discernment of distinguishing between that which is an assignment for your life and that which is mere fascination with a thing. Stability is a virtue that must be practiced and developed. When your mind and heart are single, you will *decide* and *do!* Let the Word of God create a singleness of mind and heart within you.

Mastering Decision-Making

Isaiah 30:21, *New International Version,* says, "Whether you turn to the right or to the left, your ears will hear a voice behind you, saying, "This is the way; walk in it." When using the Word of God as the basis of focus for your life, it guides you to a place where you are able to make proper decisions without regard for circumstances or the opinions of others. Those who criticize you for your decision-making are usually those who are not making decisions for their own lives.

James 1:5-7 says: "If any of you lacks wisdom, let him ask of God, who gives to all liberally and without reproach, and it will be given to him. But let him ask in faith, with no doubting, for he who doubts is like a wave of the sea driven and tossed by the wind. For let not that man suppose that he will receive anything from the Lord."

Verse 7 says, "For let not that man suppose that he will receive anything from the Lord." Who is that man? It's the man in verse 6; the man who, instead of asking in faith, wavers. It's the wavering man. What does it mean to *waver*? It means being double-minded, indecisive, and not having the ability to make clear decisions.

When one suffers from the lack of decision-making in his or her life, not much gets accomplished. I am of the opinion that this type of individual should begin to practice decision-making on a small scale so that, in life, they may become more proficient in larger and more significant decision making. This practice will help you overcome certain fears associated with decision making, including the fear of being rejected or not being liked, or the fear of commitment. Some put their lives and destinies on hold because of such fears.

Many times, we error on the side of trying to get it right by consulting with multiple voices. Somehow, we feel the more people we talk to about a matter the better chance we have of reaching the right conclusion. The Bible says in Proverbs 11:14, "Where *there is* no counsel, the people fall; but in the multitude of counselors *there is* safety." The *New Living Translation* says, "there is safety in having many advisers." The problem, though, is when there are too many people speaking in your ears, especially if half of them are not even the right people; it makes it virtually impossible for you to hear from God. When God speaks to your spirit, His Word provides two dimensions of clarity: Clarity for each step you take, and clarity for the path you're on. Psalm 119:105 says, "Thy word *is* a lamp unto my feet, and a light unto my path." The lamp shines on every step, and the light illuminates every path.

Again, practice is key to hearing properly. If you practice communicating with God, you will become proficient in it. You will discern His voice more accurately and more readily. The more this phenomenon occurs in your life, the less you will rely on the voices of those around you.

It's good to get a second opinion, and sometimes even a third or fourth. But make sure those you seek for counsel are people who have God's wisdom—that know His voice and will provide sound, godly counsel. Just because a person holds a place of endearment in your life, or because they seem to hold the secrets to success in a particular area of life, does not necessarily qualify them to give you counsel.

As a child of God, you are responsible to seek the counsel of those who are also spiritual-minded, not carnal-minded. The nature of the carnal mind suggests that reality is based on that which you can see with your natural eye. It also suggests that logic, reason, and intellect are sufficient for you to make decisions for your life.

The problem with this kind of thinking is that the Bible says in Romans 8:6-7, *Amplified Bible, Classic Edition*: "Now the mind of the flesh [which is sense and reason without the Holy Spirit] is death [death that comprises all the miseries arising from sin, both here and hereafter]. But the mind of the [Holy] Spirit is life and [soul] peace [both now and forever]. [That is] because the mind of the flesh [with its carnal thoughts and purposes] is hostile to God, for it does not submit itself to God's Law; indeed it cannot."

Preserving Focus

In James 3:13-16, *The Message*, we read: "Do you want to be counted wise, to build a reputation for wisdom? Here's what you do: Live well, live wisely, live humbly. It's the way you live, not the way you talk, that counts. Mean-spirited ambition isn't wisdom. Boasting that you are wise isn't wisdom.

Twisting the truth to make yourselves sound wise isn't wisdom. It's the furthest thing from wisdom—it's animal cunning, devilish conniving. Whenever you're trying to look better than others or get the better of others, things fall apart and everyone ends up at the others' throats."

Let's consider three things that are guaranteed to help us preserve our focus.

1. Avoid Strife

If we want to preserve our focus, we must avoid strife. Strife is like a cancer. It's not contagious, but once it's contracted it spreads. Strife will prevent the flow of God's Word in and through you, because God cannot work in an atmosphere of strife. If you are in strife with someone, pray and ask God to help you to create an opportunity for peace to be established between you.

Some situations may require that you confront the person with whom you are in strife. It's important that you do this ONLY under the strict guidance of the Holy Spirit. The truth is, in most cases, you simply must allow the Word to change the way you're thinking about that individual or that situation. This means that confrontation may not be necessary, because the problem is mostly in how you're thinking or perceiving another person or situation.

Whatever the case, it's important that strife be eradicated. James 3:16 says, "For where envying and strife is, there is confusion and every evil work" (*King James Version*). Wherever there is strife, there is confusion. No focus can occur where strife is allowed to fester.

2. Embrace Forgiveness

Embrace forgiveness, and let go of any unforgiveness you may be harboring.

Ephesians 4:32 says, "And be ye kind one to another, tenderhearted, forgiving one another, even as God for Christ's sake hath forgiven you" (*King James Version*). Unforgiveness clouds your thinking and keeps you from having clarity of heart and intent. It contaminates your focus and preoccupies your mind with things other than your assignment. Leadership requires a capacity that empowers you to release others from harm rendered toward you. The most powerful thing you can do for yourself and your future is forgive. Just let it go!

Mark 11:25-26 sums it up: "And whenever you stand praying, if you have anything against anyone, forgive him, that your Father in heaven may also forgive you your trespasses. But if you do not forgive, neither will your Father in heaven forgive your trespasses."

3. Overcome Offense

First Peter 3:8-9 says, "*be ye* all of one mind, having compassion one of another, love as brethren, *be* pitiful, *be* courteous."

It's difficult to offend someone, or to be offended when you are walking in the love of God. It's like being insulated—shielded from anything that could cause you to say or do anything that would result in hurt or harm, either to yourself or someone else. When allowed to settle in your spirit, offense will rob you of your focus. Don't let that happen. Avoid offense by staying connected to God. Decide in advance that you're going to be like Jesus—that you will say and do only what you hear and see your heavenly Father say and do. Do that, and you will overcome any level of offense in your life.

As you practice the discipline of focus, the fruit of your labor will begin to manifest before your eyes and the eyes of those observing you. You will grow and increase. As you start your journey of becoming highly developed in this spiritual attribute, you will find that you are more inclined to be organized and efficient.

Practicing focus will develop your capacity to expedite the arrival of those things you're hoping for. Find your focus, develop your focus, and protect your focus!

Prayer of Salvation

The Father's plan of salvation through Christ is a decision on your part to yield to His Lordship in your life. The following prayer is the biblical basis for such a quality decision (Romans 10:9-10). After praying this prayer, it is imperative that you allow the Father to lead you to a "Bible-teaching" church that believes in the ministry of the Holy Spirit. If you will get involved in and connected to that church, you will grow and flourish (Psalms 92:13). Pray this prayer:

"Dear Lord, I come to You now just as I am. You know my life and how I have lived. Thank You for forgiving me as I repent of my sins. I believe that Jesus Christ is the Son of God, and that He died for my sins and was the Resurrection for my redemption. Now, I yield to You. Live Your life through me. I receive the gift of Your Holy Spirit. From this day forward, I belong to You! In Jesus' Name, Amen!"